The Invisible Suitcase

poems by

Elaine E. Olund

Finishing Line Press
Georgetown, Kentucky

The Invisible Suitcase

Copyright © 2020 by Elaine E. Olund
ISBN 978-1-64662-347-1 First Edition
All rights reserved under International and Pan-American Copyright Conventions. No part of this book may be reproduced in any manner whatsoever without written permission from the publisher, except in the case of brief quotations embodied in critical articles and reviews.

ACKNOWLEDGMENTS

Thanks to the literary journals where the following poems appeared, sometimes in different form:

Peregrine: "Suppression" (Fall 2018 issue)
Turk's Head Review: "Pennsylvania" (November 2014)
everywritersresource.com: "Fossils" (December 2014)
Cosumnes River Journal: "Under an Empty Sky" (Spring 2019 issue)
Stonecrop Magazine: "Technicolor Berry" (Spring 2019 issue)
Flyway: Journal of Writing & Environment: "Watching Carnations Wilt" won first prize for Poetry in Iowa State's 2019 Sweet Corn Literary contest, appearing in publication (Summer 2019). "Food Desert" and "Thoughts While Slicing Berries" won honorable mentions in Iowa State's 2018 Sweet Corn Literary contest, appearing in publication (Summer 2018)
The Ocotillo Review: "It's Copper" (Volume 2, No. 2. May 2018)

Publisher: Leah Huete de Maines
Editor: Christen Kincaid
Cover Art: Elaine E. Olund
Author Photo: Paul Kroner
Cover Design: Elaine E. Olund

Order online: www.finishinglinepress.com
also available on amazon.com

Author inquiries and mail orders:
Finishing Line Press
P. O. Box 1626
Georgetown, Kentucky 40324
U. S. A.

Table of Contents

Gravitropism 1

Suppression 2

Pennsylvania 3

Fossils 4

Under an Empty Sky 5

Nine Little Seeds 7

Phototropism 9

Technicolor Berry 10

Food Desert 11

An Elegy to a Time I Cannot Possibly Remember 13

Letting Go 15

Dating Again 16

Thoughts While Slicing Berries 17

Marcescence 19

Tell Me a Story 20

Figuring it Out 21

It's Copper 23

Watching Carnations Wilt 25

Living Alone 27

Then the Fires Came 28

Packing List for a New Life 30

*To all my beloveds, near and far, present and past, found and lost.
From each of you I learned that home is now.
Real love never dies—it simply relocates.*

Gravitropism

Roots tunnel the earth, holding
on so tight, burrowing down
pulled by the dark magical
tug of the earth's beating heart
buried deep, that magnetic,
invisible force. Roots bind—
keep us from washing away.

Suppression

These are not tears, you see
(because you won't)
this is the sea, like an ocean
held back behind my dammed eyes

I was restrained by your—
quiet suppression
dried up as driftwood beached

but later

I began to leak, creaky old boat
of my body caught in
turning tides, neap tides, high tides

pulled, pulled, pulled by a yellow moon
a moon the size of a six-bedroom house
a moon who never gave up

pulling at tears
buried grief toxic,
suppressed

(untouchable like me)
like radioactive waste
wheeled deep into a salt mountain, hidden

but everything

leaks out over time
changes the color of the sea, blooming red:
you cannot hold back the tides

Pennsylvania

Turnpike stretches,
endless, bleached asphalt scar
beneath morning sun, stretches
into mountains
Blue, Kittatinny, Allegheny—
one by one they swallow me whole
plunge me into darkness,
spit me back into daylight.

On this rolling green ocean
ridge tops crest like rogue waves
rising up from soft valleys
rippling with corn tassels.

I think of wind, of water
of how even the earth is always moving,
rippling over time
and of how I might ripple.

Crossing Fortune Teller Creek
questions roil—
air-conditioner blasting, tears
falling, sunglasses steaming—
there's no way around it, only through—
turnpike stretches on forever
through sharp red rocks cut deep
and slowly, slowly bleeding.

Fossils

Look at the ginkgo leaves,
scattered like footprints on the
wet sidewalk, shaped like duck's feet
rubber-ducky yellow, like childhood.
Sometimes I can't remember things
sometimes I can't forget.

My memories are fossilized deep
in the muddy layers of my brain—
some shake right out, easy as trilobites,
but the ones I really want elude me,
Cretaceous, older than ancient, formed in dark
pre-cataclysmic times.

You can't kill some things.
They live on and on and on, sharp as a rock
in your shoe while you walk,
like dinosaurs walked, over ginkgo leaves.
After the bombing of Hiroshima, six charred ginkgos remained,
refusing to die—some things just won't.

Still, some things can't be preserved or kept;
the flowers the girls pressed long ago
in the M's of the unabridged dictionary
fall to powder at my touch—
some things are just too much—
fall apart, too much.

Under an Empty Sky

I dream again of the strawberry fields
the ones near Pajaro Dunes, in the fruit bowl of California,
a desert forced to kneel down and bloom—
silvery apparatus wheeling across the fields spraying water
rainbow streams in the sun
dozens of workers, dark-haired, brown-skinned
many just children,
though my brother insists they are all just so short,
short is all, no one lets children pick strawberries
but even so, they seem so small, in the dream,
crouching in the heat of the dry rows watered yesterday
plucking one by one berries sun-dried
red and glistening as a bloody nose.

Pajaro means 'bird' in Spanish, but here:
no birds, no bees, no mosquitoes, no flies, even—
just an empty summer sky
and the sound of the highway—

in the dream we stop at the wooden shack
at the intersection of two dusty farm roads
buy three pints for three dollars

three pints full
they smell sweet

delicate little miracles
plump and round as angel's hearts
and our mouths water—we want
to devour them right there

but the ghost of my sister suddenly appears
(even though she is not dead)
chiding us
to wait, wait

wash them clean with tears
and pray for forgiveness
three times
before we eat.

Nine Little Seeds

1 | Roots
The cutting in the windowsill vase
is shooting out roots
but it cannot grow there forever

2 | Fur
Cordelia is striped, like a tyger burning bright
descendant of some fierce African wildcat
trapped now in domesticity

3 | iPhone
Black glass gleams like your eyes once gleamed
I touch the screen: it lights up with words and worlds away
I think of mirages on hot July highways

4 | Coffee
Bittering now, sitting alone on the ledge
waiting to be held again in my hands
longing to be swallowed in my mouth

5 | Highlighter
Neon-yellow, it seeks and finds what
should be remembered, the important bits
is the rest really forgettable? Unimportant?

6 | Quilt
Grape-jelly purple, my round babies
once sighed and slept beneath you, warm…
Sometimes I see you breathe

7 | Berry
Stray, lost, dried-up scarlet berry
remnant of Christmas past
(it's almost April)

8 | Sketch
She's playing the sonata forever
her left foot pedals, her fingers fly
I still hear the music

9 | Lintbrush
Lurking like an aunt before the funeral
descending to pick away any flaws
I feel judged

Phototropism

There's a word for everything
this one means "grow toward light."
Plants tend to keep life simple—
born with a mission, they sprout,
burst from their seeds knowing how
they might blossom, but not why—
no questions asked, they just grow.

Technicolor Berry

Blushing and round, destined
never to reproduce, never to run wild
lithe and vine-y like the feral strawberries webbing
my backyard, berries so tiny
they're all seed.

I pop one in my mouth
lip-pucker tart crunch of seeds pincushioned
to a slip of bitter flesh—
so unlike you, California's finest
big as a plum, grown for my pleasure,

sown in fields where nothing at all runs wild
where machines spray rain onto soil
fumigated with poison, spawning tender jumbos
plucked by human hands
only because you are too tender

to be plucked mechanically.
I slice you, sacrificial berry-lamb
stainless blade halves your weeping red heart
bred to slake my desire to sink deep
into toothsome depths, so red, so red—

you taste like Technicolor cricket-singing summers
like sparkler smoke clouding stars.
You taste like I did at five, shining in my smocked dress
melting like a popsicle in the sun
when the world seemed a safe place to spin and run.

Food Desert

I'm helping Lydia water
the greens: kale, collards, red-veined chard,
parsley, turnips, cilantro

North Philly slumps around us
crumbling bricks and falling cornices
boarded up double-hung windows next to flim-flam-flash

student housing tossed up cheap in a month,
trash palaces that won't last a decade.
I feel eyes watching,

look up—polka dots and sunhat,
an elderly lady, peering through chain link:
I meet her eyes, smile—

"Ya'll ever sell those greens?" she asks.

"No, they're free," answers Lyd,
long fingers dug into dirt, voice warm
as the spring afternoon.

"Come in, we'll help you pick what you need!"

But still, the old woman hesitates
finally tiptoes in, as if she's trespassing here, ready to run,
dark eyes drinking in overflowing beds, a tender feast—

Lush oblong isle in a sea of buckled blacktop,
the garden's abuzz with bees, daisies nod heavy in the breeze,
orange butterflies soak up sunshine.

"It's all free, for the neighborhood," says Lydia.
The lady shakes her head. "Only with you here," the lady says.
"Only with you here. The campus police…"

Along the fence line, strawberry vines run, fruiting
white-green now, I imagine the berries swelling up,
blushing bloodred in June, hanging heavy in the heat

I imagine this desert grandma, after we've gone on home—
watching this bounty bolt and rot, imagine it
guarded like gold, by campus cops.

An Elegy to a Time I Cannot Possibly Remember

Dear Sister,
You are leaning over my playpen
in a sun-yellow dress, scowling
your hair is white, the color of the
bleached crib sheets, but shiny, shiny
like the nylon bristles of the brush Mama
is pulling through your hair

your hair—the brush—pale shimmery
tinged golden, just warm enough
to hint to blonde

Dear Sister,
Today you are pushing my stroller
hot-noon, up and down the driveway
our Mama is asleep on the patio hammock
dozing under drippy pines
I cannot possibly remember this, you'd say
but I do—it plays crackly like an old-time movie
in color, though,
like when the Wizard of Oz
turns vivid:

your starched pinafore
a shade paler than your hair
I see gingham-checked blue and white
fabric-covered buttons marching over your shoulders

Dear Sister,
Your Polly Flinders is smocked across
your beating heart, little orange buttons
dotting the zigzag web of embroidery
green floss, orange shine, creamy cotton

dyed the color of marmalade
you radiate, I turn toward you
like a flower opening, I reach, I reach
"Go away!" you say.
Mama is looking gray-tired
lost in a haze of Parliament smoke
I smell burnt coffee, I reach for you, I reach—

Dear Sister,
It's a church day, I think?
Yes, Palm Sunday?
I squirm as you struggle to fasten
a row of little pearly buttons
on my hand-me-down crochet sweater,
the one with a stain
from the juice you long-ago spilled
the grape-juice holy ghost
of Easter past

You scowl, frustrated at the tiny buttonholes
tiny slippery buttons
but it is a church day, Mama calls hurry up
we are supposed to look a certain way
just so, buttoned up
happy in our fine clothes
I am only two and already I feel so stiff
we both want to cry
(maybe I do)—

Dear Sister,
Do you remember this, too?

Letting Go

I thought it was you, but—

it was the future that dragged me around
flinging me this way and that
like a game of crack the whip
like we used to play in New Jersey on the January lakes

I was always the end of the whip
always flying off
always getting hurt

but before the letting go
when my little mittened hand
lost its grip on the gloved hand
of my friend—oh before that, pure joy!

speed, speed, a blur of laughter and frosty air
red and navy and lime parkas and scarves
spinning spinning the thin blue sky dome
low clouds swirl the taste of cocoa warm on my tongue

before letting go, it was like that
one moment connected, hands clasped: a pair
sliding through life and the next—
sailing across an abyss

alone, that long slide alone
skating again, heart open
we are made for this, I think? for letting go
for falling, slipping, sliding

for spin and speed and stupor
for freeze that burns
for getting back up, again

Dating Again

After the film at the Mariemont,
he licks a spoonful of mocha chip,
asks, "So, do you think that movie means—
all men just want a mother?"

I wipe his chin, murmur "of course not."

Thoughts While Slicing Berries

Sometimes, I don't think of you at all,
unless I see you.
Then, I want you—
want to have you, like a bowlful of strawberries
fresh from the icebox,
berries red as angel's hearts, and as sweet—
(the refrigerator hums, soft, like our moans in the dark)

I'm simple—c'mon, I've told you that
on our second date, when you said
your inner vixen and inner puritan were at war
with the rest of you,
I asked: how many of you are in there?
you laughed, said we all have so many sides, yes?
No, I insisted. No.
I just have the one.

In bed Sunday morning you asked if I'd do something
—special—just for you, during the week
my heart began to thump—thinking of possibilities,
but instead you asked if I'd please call to say goodnight,
because it would feel like a warm hug
I laughed—tickled you with my chin,
offered to come round midweek…

I'm just simple—I've told you that
sometimes, I don't think of you at all
sometimes, I want you, other times, not
sometimes, I think of nothing whatsoever—
while slicing these little hearts wide open
berries, I mean.

Sometimes, life washes over me like
water through a colander and I let it run, run
fingers wet numb
because when I'm cold enough—

sometimes, I can forget the burning, burning
of all I've had and lost,
had and lost, had and lost.

Marcescence

Sometimes we hold on too hard;
cling to what should be released—
old, winter-worn, transparent
from time and weather, rattled,
beaten, tattered— it's hard to
let the familiar fall
away, let new growth emerge.

Note: Marcescence is a botanical term that refers to trees that retain withered leaves over the winter. Beeches and some oaks are among the trees that cling to old dead leaves. Though there are several theories, there doesn't seem to be agreement on why this happens. One school of thought is that beeches and other marcescent trees are still evolving from evergreen to deciduous, caught forever betwixt and between two states.

Tell Me a Story

You say, and I begin again.
The beginning, always my favorite part
sweet on my tongue, fleeting

but I am ever hopeful
digging now for middles and ends
that are deeper and darker

boiling with life, like the depths
where lampreys sway like seaweed,
and dance with the current

swallowing the silvery trout
who swims too deep—
you might say the trout dies

or you might say they become one?
There is no ending, is there?
It's all a loop, this story—

as endless as the sea evaporating
graying blue skies, falling again, rain, rain
pocking the choppy waves

feel the spray on your face, wet as
the spit in your mouth, the blood in your veins
salty as the tears brimming

below the surface, unshed, submerged.
Tell me please, what really separates above from below?
If I dive in, will you swallow me whole?

Figuring it Out

After long division,
comes basic geometry
I was obtuse,
you, acute—
we both wanted
so badly to be right

in the misty aftermath
I helped at the homework lab,
relearning what I missed
in grade four—
simple things:
a line has arrows
capping both ends, indicating
an infinite path

a segment, on the other hand,
is a little chunk
part of a line
drawn with dots that look
like bullet holes
precise points
beginning,
ending

a ray, I discovered,
starts from a point—
(a smile in a library, perhaps?)
and extends on forever through mesas
crowned with sagebrush, red-dirt pathways
kisses and time opening like the starry desert sky,
no end in sight, an arrow running

for months. For years
I thought we were a ray, shining into
the dark tunnel of always
but now I understand
we were two segments,
weren't we?
just segments,
separate but running parallel
close enough to hold hands and laugh
as we headed toward the inevitable ending
it's just basic math, I see that now.

It's Copper

Remember how you asked me?
And I could never decide? Well. I've decided.
Copper is my favorite color.
Like the copper-topped table, in my kitchen. Remember it?

How do you describe a color, except to compare it to other things?

I want to describe it for a person who cannot see,
cannot conjure a shiny new penny or a spoonful of cumin.
The copper I love is the smell of orange-spice tea,
and the sound of Neil Young's original recording of "Cinnamon Girl."

Copper is the place where I could be happy, the rest of my life

Copper is the echo of the sob that last afternoon,
when this table watched me lose my compass bearings
watched as you hugged me close, asked, "what's wrong?"
though surely you knew,

in that way you have that is warm and cool all at once

Warm enough to sink into and cool enough to reflect back,
a fine trick, that, one I miss.
When I say "trick" that diminishes it, doesn't it?
Makes it grow smaller, makes it spin away
like a penny rolling into a gutter,
shining far away, no longer worth reaching for.

Lost, what was once warm in my hand, lost

But it wasn't a penny. It wasn't a trick. It was a gift,
even and maybe especially that last moment, the vibrations
of which were absorbed by this copper table
that holds my journal now as you held me that last day
that is receding, rolling away, into a place beyond sight, beyond touch—

A coppery place the color of New Mexican mesas
and freshly minted trust

It's copper—
my favorite color.
I forgot to tell you,
and now it's too late.

Watching Carnations Wilt

So white. Dirty-edged though, like snow
charcoaled with car exhaust

Pale creamy, smooth as baby's skin
as my skin was once
when azaleas bloomed under Spanish moss

I remember being a baby, do you?
Remember being a seed and also, an egg—
apart and then: collision.
Remember rooting endless rooting
then pang, pull, push, tug?

So white, tight-ruffled bud smelling sweet
like my mother's lotioned hands almond-cherry

I remember having a baby, too.
Wonder if you remember being planted deep
in-dwelling, then emerging?
How you pushed like a June lily, stargazer
sunny-side up?

I remember you, pollen on your nose
crawling in the dark loam
singing to the peonies, soprano songs
gone, gone, like you are gone,
800 miles off under a hotter sun—

So white, gathered tight as an apron edge
mama frying up eggs, bacon on the breeze

I remember being held tight, do you?
Remember being a melon swelling belly
remember kicking my way out.

So white, deckled like old photographs, the ones silvering
now in drawers, dirty-edged from fingers and time

I remember letting go, do you?
Remember bolting, blowing seedy in the breeze
a flurry, like snowflakes, falling, falling.

Living Alone

Dear tulip, drinking sun
how wonderful it feels to know love
that feeds and delights—
how I wish I could slip
between your silky petals
rest in your red-tinged darkness

it's midnight, dear tulip
do you worry the sun won't return?
(please tell me the darkness always ends)

I must tell you, dear tulip
the glow on your curves
the way you and the light—
reach and reach for one another
across millions of miles
gives me hope for I sometimes fear

some dark morning your faithful lover
will not burst pink in the east
(please tell me the darkness always ends)

I must confess, dear tulip
I'm scared of dying alone
so hold me, please, in your sweet depths
let me hide here while you tell me again, again
the story of how once you froze, cold oblivion
while the sun raced across the stars and sky—

just to touch you this morning

Then the Fires Came

So much for strawberries
it's all over now, swallowed in red-dirt desert
mirages, swirling swaying like burning trees gleaming
radiant in the dark, hot as your fevered hand in mine, burning
parched, I dreamed of water
misting cool a silver veil

like my bridal veil
shroud for my young face, lips plump strawberries
cheeks smooth still as still water
still water, a puddle mirroring sky, desert
cool inch-deep oasis, glittering distant burning
far away I see skyscrapers yet untouched, gleaming

distant windows beckoning, lit like your eyes gleaming
before the muddy veil
fell graying blue, smothering breath, something was burning
but not for me—I sigh, remembering the taste of strawberries
sweetly filling me, I'm empty now, dry like this desert
empty—rationed sips of ashy water

water, once, water everywhere—water
the blue of childhood, chlorine gleaming
concrete pool deck solstice-hot desert
my wet footprints vanishing into June's sunny veil
snack-bar popsicles dripping, grape and strawberry
tears at closing time, left behind, face red, burning

burning, now burning cars, houses, decades, burning
rising and falling like the devil's sea water
orangey-red, like strawberries
memories of me-you-us swirl in a gleaming
dreaming, gauzy veil
snapping like a sail over wind-swept desert

green-gold fields and forests char dark into desert
redwoods and succulents burning, burning
choked smoke-stung screams; downcast eyes veil
so many lost foamy hopes; puddled water
steams to vapor; fire crackles—alive, gleaming
eating the air, the birds, the sky, the strawberries

strawberries cannot bloom in the desert;
gleaming hearts, ghosts now—paradise is burning
tears water faraway eyes, sooty windswept stinging veil

Packing List for a New Life

Into the invisible suitcase, breath folded
neat as a silk scarf, sweet oxygen
deep inhalation, exhalation

and almonds, California almonds, for protein
and magnesium and blood sugar stability
(because you need energy for these things)

the crib quilt, yes, the purple crib quilt,
cheap, from Target, threadbare but still—
you can tuck that quilt around you

those endless nights, and remember the way
in the old life, you watched your babies sleeping
their chests rising, falling, rising, falling.

Thank You

Deep gratitude to Pauletta Hansel for her guidance and encouragement in and out of her Poetry Manuscript class, and to my fellow classmates for helping me shape this chapbook. Many of these poems germinated or blossomed in writing communities and workshops in Cincinnati, Ohio, Abiquiu, New Mexico and Bloomington, Indiana. Thanks to Laurie Lambert at Women Writing for (a) Change in Cincinnati for a warm place to write in community; to Joan Logghe, Susan Weber and Dona Bolding at Ghost Ranch in New Mexico for a week that opened the poetry gates and changed my life, and to Gabrielle Calvocoressi and my classmates in her Poetry Workshop at the IU Summer Writer's Conference, who treated me as an equal even though I wasn't; I learned so much from you all, and am excited to keep learning from everyone I write with.

Thanks to my most beloveds, who listen deeply and egg me on in all I do. I am so lucky.

Elaine Olund moved around a lot as a child and found her home in words and pictures. A professional designer by trade, she writes every chance she gets. As a certified yoga teacher and Amherst Writer's and Artist facilitator she loves offering yoga & writing workshops in her adopted hometown of Cincinnati, Ohio. An award-winning writer, her poetry, essays, and fiction have appeared in *Flyway: Journal of Writing & Environment, Peregrine, Stonecrop Magazine, The Ocotillo Review, Dunes Review, Black Denim Lit* and other publications. Find more of her writing at *elaineolund.com*.

www.ingramcontent.com/pod-product-compliance
Lightning Source LLC
LaVergne TN
LVHW041604070426
835507LV00011B/1301